A Few Words
in Defense of Excellence

Saying No to Comfortable Underachievment -
Why Winning is a Morally Desirable Goal
in Youth and High School Athletics

by L. Scott Swanson

ISBN 978-0-9830339-1-2

L. Scott Swanson
Write The World Right LLC
3636 S. Straits Highway / PO Box 579
Indian River MI 49749
Email - editor@resorter.com
Phone - 231-238-7362

Printed in the United States of America
1st Printing

Introduction

The most damaging problem in youth athletics today isn't the thought that you must win at all cost, it's the unfortunate and widespread notion that it's perfectly acceptable to lose at no cost.

Granted, the stereotypical, overzealous, ranting, raving parents and coaches, as short on decorum and civility as they are long on volume and bluster, are out there, but at least they're wolves in wolves' clothes, easily identified and recognized as a hazard. More dangerous and prevalent in current times are the well-intended parents, coaches and school administrators who mistake high expectations for oppression and view dedication and hard work as unwarranted suffering. Rather than providing young athletes guidance and direction, they offer affirmation and comfort. They offer affirmation by providing excuses when work is avoided followed by comfort when avoiding work leads to failure.

Berating young athletes and treating them as though their value in life is based only on stardom and their win/loss record is a message with obvious harm. But praising young athletes when there is no meaningful accomplishment and laying the groundwork for them to go through life as comfortable losers does them no favors. Fortunately, this isn't an either/or situation. There are alternatives. There's a better way.

Many adults and players involved in athletic programs realize that succumbing to the forces of mediocrity is the wrong thing to do, but they're not sure how to fight these forces. The forces of mediocrity often are difficult to identify, let alone defeat. On the surface they may appear noble, kind and warm, the approach that makes kids happy - at least in the short term. However, if you go below the surface and analyze the forces of mediocrity you find that in the long term there are sad consequences for not just the young athlete, but for the society in which he or she is a citizen. You also find that even in the short term any happiness is a thin veneer over a thick core of frustration.

The purpose of this book is to serve as a call to arms and a coat of arms for those players, coaches and parents who are frustrated by the damages of the forces of mediocrity in youth athletics. The goal of winning does not excuse bad behavior, yet that does not mean that winning must be associated with or result from bad behaviour. Quite the contrary, winning is a morally desirable goal. Coaches and other adults who have high expectations and encourage young athletes, correcting them when necessary, so that they may maximize their potential and find out just how great they can be are a good influence. Too often dedication, commitment, effort, the development of a lifelong work ethic, personal growth, winning and the people who espouse the value of these things are being discounted, excused away and in some instances outright vilified by people interested only in expedience and short term comfort. It's time that stopped. Those who truly care about young athletes must not let the forces of mediocrity prevail. This book looks at the identity and origins of these forces and provides arguments as to why they should be rejected in favor of approaches that lead an athlete to more success both on and off the court. In a nutshell, this book offers "A Few Words in Defense of Excellence."

Table of Contents

Letter 5: All Men are Created Equal, but All Athletes Aren't

Paul - 5: It's amazing how many things other than performance people contend should be used as criteria for allocating playing time. Where do these strange notions come from?

J.W. - 5: The Declaration of Independence tells us, "All men are created equal." Even if all men are created equal, all athletes certainly aren't. If you intend to have your team win, the better athletes will have to play more. Every person has the lead role in the play that is his or her own life, but an athletic season is not that play and most roles will be supporting.

Letter 6: Internal vs. External Competition

Paul - 6: What are legitimate factors to consider in allocating playing time?

J.W. - 6: External versus internal competition. If you're not willing to have hard, fair internal competition, you will not fare well against external competition.

Letter 7: Get with the Program

Paul - 7: You don't have to be involved with athletics for very long before it becomes obvious that the common denominator among great coaches is great players. How do I develop great players?

J.W. - 7: Any coach could win with players like that, but not just any coach can put together a program that produces players like that. Teach players not just to play, but to play the right way. Make playing the right way mandatory, not optional.

Letter 8: Correction is an Act of Love

Paul - 8: How does a coach make demands in a way that players will accept and respond to?

J.W. -8: Proverbs says, "It's the child He loves that God corrects." Coaches must correct players. Both coaches and players must understand that correction is not an act of hostility, but an act of love.

Letter 9: Building the Players,
Rather than the Problems of Tomorrow

Paul - 9: What about communication between the varsity coach and coaches at developmental levels? How do you keep the system connected?

J.W. - 9: A system means there are certain core things done at the varsity level and all feeder teams build toward these core things. For the varsity program, feeder programs are either eliminating problems before they get to the varsity level or creating problems that manifest themselves at the varsity level.

Letter 10: Responsibility & Authority
must be in the Same Place

Paul - 10: Sometimes players, parents and others don't want to go down the path the coach has chosen. Then what?

J.W. - 10: Responsibility and authority must be in the same place. If a coach is given the responsibility to make a program successful, he must also be given adequate authority to make and enforce decisions necessary for that to happen. One person steers the ship, not to inflate his ego, but because that's his role. Many people with hands on the wheel won't steer the ship better; they will only create confusion.

Letter 11: Terms of Participation

Paul - 11: How do you deal with kids quitting, not playing, waffling about playing or becoming ineligible or suspended?

J.W. - -11: Terms of participation are less about kids and more about the integrity, credibility and character of adults who deal with kids through athletics. Player lack of commitment and misbehavior, like losing, is often due to a defective program culture.

Letter 12: If Everybody's Perfect, How Can there be Losers?

Paul - 12: How do you deal with players who have an exaggerated opinion of their ability and also a sense of entitlement?

J.W. - 12: We live in age where people think they deserve much for doing little. The concept of winners and losers is difficult to rectify with an "everybody's perfect" philosophy of life.

Letter 13: The Reality of Athletes' Parents

Paul -13: A favorite subject of all coaches: What is the role of parents in an athletic program?

J.W. - 13: Understand that parents will focus on their own kids. Just don't allow that focus to be to the detriment of their own kid or other kids on the team. Discourage parents from subscribing to the "Glory Days" mentality. Although almost every coach has stories of parents who are difficult to deal with, the majority of parents are good people.

Letter 14: Yes, Tactics are Important

Paul - 14: Can we talk a bit about tactics? What about the X's and O's?

J.W. - 14: X's and O's are important, just not of primary importance. Build a sound foundation before you build the house. If there was one perfect offense or defense, then all great teams would be running the same offense and defense. Imitators of trends are always one step behind. It's not what you choose to do so much as that you do what you choose to do extremely well.

Letter 15: Why Coach?

Paul - 15: Coaching requires a huge commitment of time and effort. Some people don't like you if you do it wrong. Others like you even less if you do it right. Why do it at all? What makes it worthwhile?

J.W. - 15: There are dark forces of mediocrity that would teach young people to be comfortable when they underachieve. This isn't healthy for players, parents, coaches or the long-term well being of our society. Good coaches teach players things that not only allow them to succeed in athletics, but also in life to the benefit of both themselves and society as a whole. That's worthwhile. It is an opportunity to help, to speak and act with strength and character in defense of excellence.

The Secrets to Success & Failure

Dear Uncle J.W.,

As the recently hired varsity coach for the local high school team I've been evaluating the status of the program I'm taking over. So far, one problem stands out above all others. They lose a lot. In recent years our team has fallen on hard times. I don't want to leap to conclusions and blame it all on any one thing, but I've noticed that our players don't play well. I'm thinking this may be a factor.

Despite the challenges, I harbor hopes and aspirations. Thus I'm sending out this letter, a plea for help and advice from a man who beyond being my favorite uncle also happens to be, even in retirement, a coaching legend.

I grew up watching you as you coached your teams, winning championships and enjoying so much success. The team I'm taking over is at the other end of the success spectrum. In every game one team must win and another must lose. Most of the time the "must lose" team has been us. How do I fix that?

I've been reading books, watching DVDs, cramming my brain full of skills, drills, plays and strategies. There are young children in our school system who will be learning only a portion of their alphabet this year because I've stolen all of the x's and o's.

Even as I study these things, I have a feeling there's something I'm missing. The team has had several coaches in recent years, some of them probably smarter than me, (You're not obligated to agree too quickly with that.) coaches who seemed strong enough on tactical aspects of the game. Yet most of the time their teams lost. Maybe not every year, but certainly in some of those losing years the team had players who were strong and fast. So I'm thinking there's something more, something I'm missing, something winning programs do and losing programs don't do.

I figure if anyone knows what that something is, it's you. I'm hoping you'll spill the beans on what it takes to have a successful varsity athletic program. I'm searching for the secret to success.

Seeking guidance,
your nephew Paul

Dear Paul,

When you're searching for something, rule number one is "Don't search for something that's not there."

You say you're searching for the secret to success. In discussing high school athletic teams, people often speak of the secret to success, but they never speak of the secret to failure. Perennial winners have no secret to their success. They're proud of what they do, will tell you about it, and place it prominently on display. Perennial losers are the teams that have secrets. The things they do that make them consistent losers are such closely held secrets they don't even acknowledge them to themselves.

If there is any secret to turning your program around and making it successful you don't need to look at other programs to find it, you need to look at your own program. The first step is for you and others involved with your program to be open, introspective and courageous enough to take an honest, objective look to see what things you're doing that are leading to failure. After that, you need to make the necessary decisions and take the actions required to alter the course.

This won't be easy. The status quo is never an accident. Things are the way they are because having them that way works for someone. If you're not sure who that someone is, start to change things. They'll holler.

Although retired, I'm willing to offer my insights and answer any questions that I can to help you in your efforts. Be advised, some of the actions I encourage you to take won't meet with universal approval. Some things I tell you will challenge certain beliefs that sound nice and that many well-meaning people currently involved in high school athletics and education hold sacred even though these beliefs when implemented don't teach young people the values and work ethic necessary to achieve. Instead, they teach young people how to be comfortable when they underachieve. As a result the athletic program underachieves. Worse yet, players then go forth in life and continue to underachieve.

Despite these consequences, those who believe in the view points will not be happy when you challenge them. Those who espouse the wonders of teenage self-esteem based on nothing, ascribe success unrelated to effort or accomplishment, shower awards without merit and offer hollow billowing acclaim upon any young person who shows up and has a pulse will promptly see you as a heartless ogre and a heretic when you question this behavior. But if you're willing to carry the torch that sheds light on the naked emperor I'll gladly do what I can to provide you with fuel for the flame.

In the opening of your letter you said you've been evaluating the status of the team you'll be coaching. You said that in recent years the team has fallen on hard times. How hard are the times? How many recent years? Enough so that losing has become the expected outcome?

Don't rely on people's memories and recollections to answer these questions. Fishermen's memories concerning the size of fish they caught pale in comparison to memories of coaches and players about their win-loss records from days gone by. Dig out the record books from the past 10 to 15 years and come up with actual numbers, numbers that may be "hard" in more than one sense of the word. Compare these numbers to what people have been telling you. I'll be curious to hear what you find out.

Your uncle,
J.W.

What a Team Should Be & Not Be

Dear Uncle J.W.,

Well that was an interesting assignment. I did what you told me to and looked up the actual records from past seasons. Over the past 15 years our team has won only 35 percent of their games. There were three seasons when they had a winning record, but even in those seasons there were no conference or tournament championships. In the other dozen seasons there were a couple where they were around .500, but most years our team routinely got trounced.

You encouraged me to compare the win-loss numbers to what people have been telling me. That's where things get really strange.

People around town rave about the rare winning seasons and wipe from memory all years when the team lost. In their recollections they paint such a wonderful picture. To hear people talk you'd think I'm inheriting a dynasty.

With this shared community fantasy firmly entrenched, most people aren't bothered by the program's losing. However, even though they aren't bothered by it, you'd at least think a few would be curious about why our team loses and other teams don't.

I look at the athletes our team has had over the years and it's not like there's some genetic flaw or something in the water supply that makes our young people athletically deficient. Our kids and the kids from opposing teams look similar when they arrive for the game and get off the bus. But once the two teams begin to play, you quickly see the difference. Players from winning teams know what they're supposed to be doing and do things correctly.

Our players don't.

Community members seem willing to accept losing and pretend that it's all right. However, the fact that they forget the losing seasons and only talk about the rare winning seasons leads me to believe they have no moral objection to winning. I know I certainly would prefer to have a team that wins more often than it loses. But the research you had me do makes it very clear that right now that's not what we have.

Faced with a tradition of losing and people who aren't unhappy about it, how do I change things? How do I get our program to be what I want it to be?

Your better informed, but
now more perplexed nephew,
Paul

Dear Paul,

In order to have your program to be what it should be, it must first not waste time and energy trying to be what it is not. Losing teams don't set out to purposely be bad. A losing team's first losses aren't games. The first losses are focus and the sense of purpose required to be good. Losing teams venture off down other paths.

For a high school athletic program to be successful, players, coaches, parents, school administrators and board members must first understand and embrace what a high school athletic program is and what it is not.

An athletic team is just that, an athletic team, not after-school daycare for teenagers, not a social club, not rehab, not group therapy. Players are there to be team members, learn to play a game, work to develop skills and compete to the best of their abilities. Players are not there to be entertained, rehabilitated, counseled or each individually coddled, gratified and glorified. The coach is there to be a coach, not a babysitter, not a cruise ship activity director, not a therapist, but a coach to teach, guide and direct players and make decisions that will lead the team to play the game to the best of its collective ability.

The idea that an athletic team is not after-school daycare for teenagers, a social club, rehab or group therapy might seem obvious, yet countless programs fail because people associated with the program, people who are well intended but misguided, fall into the trap of trying to make athletic programs into things they're not.

Be advised here, (and this is very important) even though these are well meaning people, when they try to make the program into things that it's not and you as a coach refuse to go that direction, their initial response will not be appreciation. You are challenging deeply held beliefs. Some of these people will look at you in bewilderment. Others will view you as evil incarnate, wondering, often aloud, have you no heart?

Before the lynch mob forms, you might want to point out to these people that your goals are the same as theirs.

Yes, we want our young people to participate in athletics after school rather than engaging in undesirable activities, be part of teams rather than gangs, steer away from harmful behaviors and toward things that are healthy and productive, feel they have the support of coaches, teammates and the broader educational system and community. There's nothing wrong with any of these goals. They are wonderful and worthy. The issue is how best to reach these goals. Some roads that look like they lead to these goals don't, while other roads, though more indirect, actually get you there.

In your previous letter you mentioned that many people in your community seem willing to accept losing. However, you also wrote that winning seasons, while rare, are the ones that community members hold in their memory and "rave about." Doesn't that strike you as inconsistent? Why, if people enjoy winning, are they not willing to do the things necessary for winning to occur on a more regular basis? If there is joy in winning that is not there when the team is losing, with what do they fill the void?

As a new coach, the first question going through your mind is "How do I get this team to win?" You've skipped too far ahead. First you have to figure out the answer to a different and more difficult question. "Why are these people comfortable losing?"

Uncle J.W.

Winning is a
Morally Desirable Goal

Dear Uncle J.W.,

You asked why people in this community are comfortable losing.

When you told me to look up the team's record over the past several years, you said not to trust people's memories because the memories of fishermen recalling the size of the fish they caught pale in comparison to coaches and players remembering win-loss records. I suspect that the same memory flaw that allows people to inflate past wins also proves useful in forgetting past losses. It's like a telescope. If you look through it correctly, things look larger. But if you turn it around and look through it backwards, things look so small that you can't even determine what they are.

In this town, a little winning is something that people will talk about for years and a lot of losing is something that's never talked about. So if all you go by is hearing people talk, you'd think there's a lot of winning.

Selective memory is one element in getting people comfortable with losing, but it's incomplete and needs an additional element to succeed over the long term. In competitive athletics there are winners and losers and records are kept. Eventually some rude and impudent person, perhaps a new coach acting on the advice of a retired uncle, will have the temerity to look up the records. He may even be so lacking in social graces that he points these records out in conversations thereby threatening the house of cards that even if built on fantasy has kept everyone happy.

Given that win-loss records are hard to deny, additional gymnastics are required to maintain the comfort level. Forgetting about losing can be done, but it takes time. In its immediae aftermath arguments must be made to validate losing and at least diminish the value of, if not outright discredit, winning. I think this relates to what you are talking about when you ask how people fill the void left by the absence of the joy that comes with winning.

Since things that are quantifiable and verifiable, like win-loss records, produce discomfort, people instead focus on things that are intangible and immeasurable and can be used to produce comfort, to fill the void you spoke of.

Participation, self-esteem, being part of a team, community support, building character, the greater goals of athletics. People in this community talk about these things a lot. They dwell on them to the point that the unspoken implication becomes that while winning would be nice, it's not necessary. Losing isn't so bad as long the team is doing well on the intangible things. Whether or not the team really is doing well on the intangible things is never scrutinized and evaluated and is supposed to just be taken as a given. If anyone were ever forward enough to question how the team is performing on immeasurable things, the conditioned reflex reply would be, "They're doing well."

No evidence would be cited to validate this response. Everybody says they're doing well so it must be true.

The team and community rarely find victory, but they find comfort. They're happy where they are. How am I supposed to persuade them that they should leave their comfort zone and trade it in for measurable achievements and accomplishments? How do I convince them that winning is worthwhile?

Looking for a strategy,
Your nephew Paul

Dear Paul,

Simplistic movies about athletics almost always include among their characters the stereotypic parent or coach who rants, raves and demeans people because he or she believes in "winning at all costs." Granted, people like that exist and they're a pain and such behavior is to be condemned and not condoned. But just because some people get obnoxious in their desire to win does not mean that it is morally wrong to have winning as a goal. Some people would seem to have us believe that winning is incongruous with the social goals of athletics. The truth is quite the opposite. While there may be a right way and a wrong way to pursue it, winning is a noble goal.

If you look around, you'll see some things that are overlooked by people who espouse social goals while acting as though winning isn't particularly desirable. If you watch and pay attention, you'll find that teams that win are not less likely, but on the contrary much more likely than losing teams to also attain the social goals. After the game, while the winning team celebrates, relives the small victories that led to the overall victory and enjoys a sense of accomplishment and a spirit of camaraderie, members of the losing team, having nothing to celebrate, point fingers in blame, feel frustrated and are anxious to put the bad memory of the game and all things and people associated with it behind them and move on to something different.

Winning may not be everything, but it's not a bad thing. Winning is more often than not a symptom of and associated with a lot of good things. The flip side of the coin is that losing is often a symptom of and associated with a lot of bad things other than just the final score.

Remember what I wrote in an earlier letter about social goals. We want our young people to participate in athletics after school rather than engaging in undesirable activities, be part of teams rather than gangs, steer away from harmful behaviors and toward things that are healthy and productive, feel they have the support of coaches, teammates and the broader educational system and community.

Which path is more likely to get you to these goals, having an athletic team be what it is, an athletic team? Or having it try to be things it is not: a social club, afterschool daycare, rehab or group therapy?

When an athletic program tries to be after school daycare, a social club, rehab or group therapy, you get losing. When you get losing, you get frustration. Young people, not wanting to be part of frustration, stop playing sports and go find something else, frequently something less desirable, to do after school. (In some instances they stay, but when they stay they make excuses. We can talk more about those later.) Losing being an unpleasant enough experience to share on the court or field, players on losing teams aren't inclined to spend any additional time with their teammates or coaches away from the game. They don't associate these people with accomplishments or good feelings. Trying to turn an athletic program into rehab, particularly through lax discipline and soft standards, only enables and reinforces problems a player has and exposes other players to the problems. Group therapy just creates a lot of drama and takes up time that could be spent more productively.

Meanwhile, when an athletic program avoids being things that it's not and instead focuses on being an athletic program, other things happen. Young people, like anyone else, want to be part of something successful. Being part of a successful winning team is a pleasant shared experience. When the experience shared with teammates and coaches on the field is pleasant, players are more willing to associate with each other in other activities. Players who need rehab don't need more excuse makers and enablers in their lives. What they need is an alternative activity under the direction of people of moral integrity and credibility who have the character and backbone to require and provide discipline and structure on a consistent basis. Young people who have problems at home or in

12

other areas of their lives don't need to come to practice and have a group therapy session to remind them about these problems. They need a safe place where they come for a few hours and work at something they enjoy and feel a sense of accomplishment. For a player who has a challenging life at home, losing just adds another frustration. Even worse is losing and conveying the message that losing is okay for that player because, given the player's circumstances, nothing more is really expected. Young people don't need that. They need demands, expectations and the inspiration to face and overcome adversity on the way to meaningful achievements. They need valid accomplishments resulting from honest and dedicated effort. These are things they can take into life and build upon.

Yes, when you have a program based on expectations and requirements rather than coddling and entitlement, tell young people and parents not what they want to hear, but what they need to hear, you will incur criticism. But consider the choice. Conduct the program in a manner that teaches players to be comfortable losers and helps set them on a path toward a lifetime of excuses and low achievement, or lead the program in a way that teaches players that success requires staying focused, making sacrifices and working hard and then see where those lessons take your players in later life. The right choice is worth the criticism.

Sending you into the fire,
Uncle J.W.

A Million Excuses
in Just Two Flavors

Dear Uncle J.W.,

So you're saying that what an athletic program is "to be or not to be," that is the question.

"To be or not to be" are the words of that particular Shakespearian speech that people remember, but there's more to the speech. If you read the whole speech it goes on to talk about suffering "slings and arrows" and taking arms against "a sea of troubles."

I understand what you're saying about people being offended when someone starts doing things they're not used to. But I've been around athletics long enough to know that if you're someone who can't take people criticizing and disagreeing with you, then coaching, or worse yet officiating, high school sports isn't something you should be doing. I'm aware there will be times when people aren't happy with me and that criticism goes with the terrain. Every coach has his detractors.

You also mentioned excuses. I find the excuses that people make more troubling than criticism. In this program, people have excuses for everything. Players have excuses for not practicing. Once they're at practice they have excuses for not practicing hard. When poor practice leads to playing poorly in games, they've got excuses for that. And it's not just the players. Parents and other adults are even worse. After a loss, if the players can't think of enough excuses, adults quickly jump in and the next thing I know I'm listening to a full blown Excuseorama. When it comes to making excuses, players are amateurs compared to some of the adults

15

around here. The adults are veteran excuse makers. They know them all and since they're adults, they think that automatically makes their excuses valid and beyond question.

After reading your letter, I have a much better idea of what I want our athletic program to be and not be, but as long as people keep making excuses, getting the program to be what it should be is going to be a challenge.

What to do? What to do?
Paul.

Dear Paul,

In war it is said that victory has a thousand fathers while defeat is an orphan. In athletics victory has a thousand fathers while defeat has a million excuses.

You're right. It's not just players who make excuses. Coaches make them, parents make them, spectators make them, administrators make them. If excuses traded as a market commodity the price would never be high because there would never be a shortage. Nobody would ever corner the market. There would always be more than enough. Yet excuses aren't a market commodity. They're just excuses and the price isn't low, it is high.

While excuses are plentiful, they come in just two flavors, "before" and "after." The before excuses are made in order to avoid things necessary to prepare to be successful, specifically time and effort. The after excuses are made in order to provide comfort when the before excuses prove effective and individuals or teams fail.

Let's look at the "before" excuses first. Ideally, if you can eliminate the excuses that keep a team from being successful, you won't have to deal with the "after" excuses because rarely does anybody feel compelled to make excuses for success. This is the "an ounce of prevention is worth a pound of cure" approach.

When players make excuses to avoid the preparation necessary to be successful it indicates that they either don't realize preparation is necessary for success or they realize preparation is necessary for success, but they also realize that preparation requires time and effort and they'd rather avoid that.

For a program to be consistently successful, players must do the things necessary to maximize their potential. Doing the things necessary to maximize their potential requires time and effort. Excuses are an attempt to escape from that reality. But there is no escaping it. Escaping from Alcatraz is a piece of cake compared to escaping from that particular reality. You can no more flap your lips and excuse your way to success than you can flap your arms and fly.

In my first letter I told you that you needed to look at your team's past records in an honest, candid way even if what you find isn't pleasant. Hopefully, you haven't put the courage and candidness required for doing that away because those traits will also be needed in responding to excuses. The best way to deal with excuses is to be honest, blunt and direct.

For example, one of my favorite excuses to respond to is that of players "just not having fun."

Some of the same people who would have athletic programs be things that they aren't also propagate the notion that the only thing truly important is that players are having fun. Excuse makers who have accepted this premise feel that the "just not having fun" excuse is not only valid, but so valid and such a trump card that any coach accused of running a program in such a way that a player is "just not having fun" has no moral alternative but to mend his ways, end the oppression and operate the program in a way that is less demanding and more fun.

However, when you think this matter through, it turns out there is an alternative response. Once you accept the premise that being successful is fun and being unsuccessful is not, the logic from there is pretty straightforward.

If a player is unsuccessful there are two possible reasons for that. Either the player lacks the raw ability to ever be successful, in which case the player is miscast even being part of the program. Or the player has the raw ability and potential to be successful, but for some reason as of yet isn't successful. If a player has the ability, but isn't successful, it's normally because the player hasn't developed the skills needed to be successful. Why hasn't the player developed the skills needed to be successful? Typically, this is because the player hasn't done the work necessary to develop those skills. Why hasn't the player done that work? Because rather than doing the work, the player has chosen to make excuses and be lazy.

Now that we've worked our way down to the root of the problem, let's reverse course and work our way up to the solution. How do we correct this situation? How does the player become successful and start having fun? Stop making excuses, get a fire under his butt, do the work to develop the skills, then put the skills to use and be successful. That will be fun.

As a coach, you should be in favor of fun. Fun is where you're trying to end up, but getting to the fun requires work not excuses.

Not accepting excuses to avoid preparation is the first step in ridding the program of the "before" excuses. The second step and one that should not be neglected is convincing players to redefine the way they view the time and effort, i.e. the work, that goes into practice. Great athletes, great musicians, great writers, great inventors, high achieving people in any field more often than not don't see doing the work and having fun as mutually exclusive. Great players, rather than fearing or disdaining practice and preparation, embrace the challenge. For them, the question is not, how much work can I avoid, it's how can I work effectively to get to be as good as I can I be?

People who own horses, if they're lucky, will have 10 percent of the time they spend with the horse be riding time. The other 90 percent is feeding, grooming, shoveling stalls etc. If you enjoy doing those things, then they're not a problem, they're just part of the experience of having a horse. If you don't enjoy those things, then you shouldn't buy a horse because you're probably going to find that the 10 percent of the time spent riding just isn't worth it.

Being on a high school athletic team is a similar proposition. For every hour of game time, there will be several hours of practice, conditioning and learning about the game. If a player doesn't enjoy those things, she probably shouldn't go out for that sport. When players embrace not just the success, but also embrace the work necessary to achieve success, excuses disappear and success is much more likely to follow.

The "after" excuses, which are excuses players and others make after a poor performance, are meant to be helpful, but they just make a bad situation worse. These are excuses people make after a contest that a team has lost even though it should have won or at least played much better. Following is a sampling of excuses you hear after games by players and other people associated with consistently losing programs. In parentheses I've included responses that shed the hard, cold light of reality on the post-loss excuses.

"We played better in the fourth quarter." (Once the other team got way ahead and emptied their bench we didn't look quite so miserable.)

"We didn't get beat by that team as bad as we did last year." (Last year's team lost by 40 points while this year's team lost by 37. At this rate in 20 more years we'll be competitive.)

"The referees were terrible. They made bad calls." (Referees may make some bad calls and on rare occasions change the outcome of a game. However those occasions are the exception, not the rule. Consistent losses by lots of points are not the result of bad calls, they're the result of bad play.)

"I don't like playing that team. They're mean." (They like playing you. You're weak.)

And from parents, the aforementioned, "As long as the kids are having fun." (Your kid is not having fun losing. If your kid is having fun losing, you should be concerned and attempt to correct that problem. Otherwise, you're setting your kid up to go out in life and be a comfortable loser. If you are a caring parent, this should not be what you want for your child.)

All of these excuses are typically made by well-intended people who only want to make the players feel better. The problem is that in order to stop losing, players don't need to feel better, they need to play better.

As a coach, when you hear these excuses you need to address the matter immediately.

Here's something to try. After a loss followed by excuses sit the players down and draw a vertical line down the middle of a white board. On the left side of the line make a list of excuses such as those mentioned above. On the other side of the line make a list that includes things such as: We need to pass better. We need to get off to a better start. We ran some plays where our timing was just a little bit off, perhaps our footwork wasn't quite right.

When you finish, you'll have two lists side-by-side. Explain to your players the difference between the two lists. The list on the left is a list that will make you comfortable losers. When you get to the point where you ignore that list and focus on the list on the right you'll be on your way to becoming winners.

One other thing that needs to be mentioned is the occasional excuse that makes sense, the valid reason, the good excuse. While their numbers pale in comparison to the lame excuses, they do exist.

There will be times when players need to miss practices or games and have valid reasons for doing so. Medical appointments, college visits and tests, family functions such as weddings, funerals. Things happen. There are times when players will have legitimate reasons for missing practices or games. At times such as these a coach needs to understand the situation. However, and this is the part that's almost always neglected and ignored, the player and parents also have to understand the situation.

Teams practice, not just to occupy time, but for a purpose. The purpose of practice is for players to develop skills, learn plays and tactics and get in proper physical condition to be ready to play the games. In games, players demonstrate the proficiencies they've developed in practice. Successful teams fare well in games because they've had valuable and productive practices.

A player who misses a practice will not be as well prepared as one who didn't miss the practice. This will be true regardless of whether the player missed the practice for a legitimate reason or for something frivolous.

Players and parents are quick to claim that it's unfair to penalize a player who has a legitimate reason for missing a practice. And they're right. However, it's also unfair to penalize the rest of the team because a player missed practice.

For example, if the coach puts in a new play during practice on Wednesday and Thursday, is the team not allowed to run that play in Friday's game because one player had to miss those two practices for a funeral? No. The team will run the play with one of the players who was at practice on Wednesday and Thursday. Does that constitute penalizing a player unfairly? No, not at all. It's not a matter of penalizing anybody. There's nothing punitive about it. It's just a matter of doing what's in the best interest of the team. At the first opportunity, the player who missed the practices will be brought up to speed. The player and the player's parents need to understand that.

Furthermore, if a player misses practice or a game, be it for a legitimate or illegitimate reason, and another player steps in and plays well, that other player is going to keep right on playing. In successful programs, playing time is performance based and not reserved.

Enough about excuses. If you're going to have a successful athletic program, the fewer excuses the better. When it comes to words that begin with "ex," teams that are successful don't have time for excuses because they're focused on and passionately pursuing excellence.

Hope this helps you,
Uncle J.W.

All Men are Created Equal,
but All Athletes Aren't

Dear Uncle J.W.

Thank you for the advice about how to handle excuses. When it comes to ridding this program of excuses I'll need all the help I can get. For decades, excuses have been the cornerstone of the program. Eliminating them will leave a big hole, a big hole that I plan to fill with something much better.

At the end of your letter you spoke of playing time being performance based and not reserved. That's a subject I need you to expand on. In a way, this is the flip side of the coin for excuses. On one side of the coin players make excuses for things they don't want to do. On the other side of the coin they claim they have a right to and are entitled to playing time. I'm absolutely amazed by the things, other than performance, people think should be used to determine playing time. They're seniors, they attend all the practices, they were good players at lower levels, their parents support the program, their parents were good players when they were in school, on and on it goes. When it comes to playing time complaints, parents are far worse than the players. Players have at least some idea of their capabilities and limitations. But some parents, when it comes to assessing their own kid's abilities and shortcomings, are in a complete fantasyland. How do I bring them back to reality?

As a coach I want every player to want playing time, but there's only so much playing time to go around. How do I allocate it?

More tricky questions,
Paul

23

Dear Paul,

Playing time is the great unequalizer.

The Declaration of Independence tells us "all men are created equal." Perhaps all men are created equal, but all athletes aren't. Some jump higher, shoot straighter, hit harder, run faster, block better and pass more accurately than others. And if you intend to have your team win, those better athletes will have to play more. The sooner this is made clear to players and parents, the better off you and the team are going to be.

A mistake some coaches make is attempting to play along with the charade that all athletes are equal. Rather than correcting this misconception, they help foster it. Then game night comes and a player who has been led to believe that all players are equal finds himself sitting on the bench while other players who he's been misled into believing he's equal to get the bulk of the playing time. What he's been told and believes are different than what he's experiencing. Not surprisingly, this causes discomfort, friction and hostility.

Instead of sowing or reinforcing the delusion that all players have equal athletic ability, a coach is better off to, even at the risk of hurting some feelings initially, be honest and tell players and parents that in terms of athletic ability players aren't equal and therefore some will get more playing time than others.

The only way in which all players on the team are equal is that each can make a contribution to the program. However, not all players are equal in terms of what that contribution will be.

While high school athletics can teach young people and community members some of the finer character traits of humanity, they also exposes some of the worst. Often these lesser character traits - a delicate ego, selfishness and deceit - surface due to quarrels over playing time.

Players and parents enjoy the spotlight and acclaim that comes from a player's individual accomplishments. This is particularly true in perennially losing programs. People involved with programs that lose year in and year out get used to focusing on individual accomplishments. One of the main reasons they do this is because there aren't any significant team accomplishments.

When the focus is on individual accomplishments, players getting the majority of the playing time may feel good about what's going on, but even that's not guaranteed. Sometimes the one good player on a bad team is good because she understands what it takes to be good and is doing what is necessary to be good. Unfortunately, nobody else on the team has the same level of talent or dedication and you end up with one good player who's getting a lot of playing time and attention, but is still frustrated.

In programs where the only accomplishments are individual, players getting limited playing time are almost invariably unhappy. They take it personally, and why wouldn't they? If a program appears to be run for the benefit of individuals rather than for the benefit of the team, then it should come as no surprise that any perceived slights are taken as slights against individuals rather than as slights against the team.

The first thing that needs to be done in order for players to stop feeling insulted as individuals over playing time is for players to stop focusing on themselves as individuals and instead focus on themselves as members of a team. That may sound like a simple, straight forward thing, but in a society that from infancy on tells young people that each of them is "special," getting these same young people to put aside their "specialness" in the interest of something such as a team isn't the easiest thing to accomplish. For their parents, it's even more difficult. As a coach, you can tell parents to try to view not just their own biological child, but all of the kids on the team as their own. Yet there's still only one kid on that team whose crib that parent stood next to, silently listening to make sure the infant was breathing.

In the end what every player and parent needs to understand and accept is that while every person has the lead role in the play that is his or her own life, the team and the season are not the play that is each player's life. It's a different play and not every role is the lead. Most roles are supporting.

Even when players understand and accept the importance of supporting roles, sometimes this is more difficult for parents because supporting roles and their value aren't especially visible.

Good parents love, care about and value their children. Not surprisingly, they also want other people to love, care about and value their children. There's nothing wrong with this. It's highly desirable. As a coach, as a decent human being, you should be all for this and encourage it.

Typically parents attend only games. They don't attend practices, don't ride the bus, aren't usually there when the team is eating lunch together, talking in the locker room or the hallway or in team meetings. When attending games, the only thing parents of a back-up player see is their son or daughter not playing as much as some of the other players. Why is that, these parents wonder? Apparently their son or daughter is not loved, cared about and valued. The parents find it difficult to understand why the player even stays on the team if he or she isn't going to do anything useful. What perplexes these parents even more is that despite limited playing time, their son or daughter not only doesn't complain, but actually seems to enjoy being part of the team. Why?

The answers to the parents' questions are in what they're not seeing. When parents see their son or daughter getting limited playing time in games, they're seeing the results of their child's weaknesses. They're not seeing other situations where their son or daughter has strengths.

There are countless players who aren't starting, but show up every day for practice, push the starting players to make them better, ask intelligent questions, possess a personality that brightens the room as soon as they walk in the door, and demonstrate a work ethic that not only great teams, but great nations are built upon.

Coaches and teammates love, care about and value players like that. But when parents are sitting in the stands at the game listening to people cheer for other players while their son or daughter is sitting on the bench, it can be difficult to see that love, care and value.

Sometimes when parents complain, a coach needs to be blunt and firm, but not always. There are times when the only thing a complaining parent needs is a little information. For parents of the star players, it's often easy to be proud of their son or daughter. For parents of role players, it might not be as easy to be proud of their son or daughter, but that doesn't mean it's not equally justified.

Here's a closing thought about individual versus team perspective.

One of the things that public school players, coaches and fans often notice is that there are a lot of nuns, priests, pastors and other religious types hanging out at the state finals. You'll hear a lot of speculation as to the reasons that parochial schools do well in athletics. They recruit. They have more money. They have a higher percentage of boys or girls among their student body therefore they should be playing in a higher class. They have divine intervention on their side.

Some or all of these things may or may not be true depending on which parochial school you're talking about. But there's something else that needs to be considered. A basic premise of almost every religion is that there is something larger than you, that you are not the most important thing, that you should put aside selfish ways and be willing to make sacrifices in service of something larger and more important than yourself, that an important part of the reward you feel is in this service.

Any team, regardless of sport, that has players and parents who have that type of belief system starts out with a huge advantage over a team that doesn't have that going for them.

In support of selflessness,
Uncle J.W.

27

Internal vs. External Competition

Dear Uncle J.W.,

I understand what you're saying about establishing a premise of being team oriented. But even if I'm able to persuade players and parents to understand and adopt that philosophy, still there are decisions that must be made regarding playing time. What factors can legitimately be used to make those decisions?

Still perplexed,
Paul

Dear Paul,

Competitive athletics are just that, competitive. There is competition that is external and competition that is internal. Games against other teams are external competition. Deciding which players get the most playing time involves internal competition. If your team cannot bring itself to participate in hard-fought, fair and objective internal competition it will never be strong enough to fare well in external competition.

Internal competition is just another way of saying that playing time must be earned through performance. It's not a right claimed through seniority, argument, pouting, parental complaints, political connections, maintaining the status quo, previous performance or inheritance. People who don't accept the team concept discussed earlier and who don't feel they're going to do well if the standard for determining playing time is performance based internal competition will make arguments for using every other standard on that list and perhaps even come up with more. Oddly enough, some coaches buy these arguments.

The seniority argument comes in two forms. One is seniority as in "I'm a senior. I deserve to play." The other is, "I was here first. If a new player arrives either through moving to the school or moving up from a lower level, I still get to play ahead of him."

In order for a coach to accept either of these arguments he first must abandon the concept of playing time being performance based and therefore also abandon any notion of having the team compete at its highest level.

If you keep performance and competition in the equation, then a player who is a senior is in a more precarious, rather than a more advantageous position regarding playing time. If a senior and an underclassman are equal in terms of ability and performance, then the underclassman rather than the senior should get more playing time. By virtue of performing as well as the senior despite having fewer years in the program, the underclassman has demonstrated a better learning curve and also indicated that with more playing time she will bypass the senior.

The argument that a player currently playing a position has squatter's rights and can't be bumped out by a better player moving in or moving up also requires performance to be discounted and diminishes the team's ability to be competitive both internally and externally. It needs to be pointed out that even though there's no guarantee of permanently occupying a position, the incumbent player does have a legitimate course of action he can pursue to decrease the possibility of being bumped. If the incumbent player is vehemently opposed to the possibility of being bumped, he's more than welcome to work really hard to minimize the chances of that happening.

Argument, pouting, parental complaints are all just different facets of the same approach. What you have is a player who can't get playing time through a performance based standard attempting to argue, pout or have parents talk the player's way onto the court. When a coach acquiesces to this type of behavior, everybody involved suffers: the program, the coach, other players and ultimately the complaining player and parents.

Obviously, the program suffers because playing a player who pouts well over one who performs well makes the program less competitive. A coach who allows players to argue or pout or parents to complain a player onto the court is going to soon suffer through a lot more of the same behavior. Once players and parents realize that's the way to get playing time, the line quickly forms. There's a simple rule that a coach needs to remember and follow, not just in regard to this issue, but also to others. If you don't want to see a behavior again, don't reward it the first time. The corollary to that rule is that good behavior must never be penalized. A player must never be passed over for playing time just because as a coach you know that player and his parents won't complain while others might.

Even the player and the parents of the player who ends up pouting and complaining his way onto the court, though rewarded in the here and now, suffer in the long term. Having mom come in and pitch a fit may get the kid playing time on the high school team, but it sets the kid up for a rude awakening in the working world. In the working world, the human resources manager has instructions to hire the best person for the job. If an applicant thinks having his mom come in and complain will trump an impressive resume and a strong interview, he's in for a very unhappy surprise.

The "previous performance" argument is based on the theory that because a player played well at a younger age level, he should also be playing well and therefore playing often at a higher age level. And if he's not, it's the coach's fault. This argument conveniently neglects that different kids grow and develop at different ages and rates. Some kids hit ninth or tenth grade and suddenly shoot upward. Other kids reach their full height by eighth grade and, much to the dismay of the high school basketball or football coach, almost seem to shrink during high school. Those are just

31

the physical things. In adolescents, the psychological and behavioral factors are also volatile. Some players either don't work as hard or work harder as they get older and that also changes the performance mix and playing time picture. Coaches need to modify playing time to adjust for these things and players and parents need to realize that's going to happen.

Many a varsity coach has had the parent of an eleventh grade player sitting on the bench say, "But my son was such a good eighth grade player."

To which the coach is tempted to reply, "And your son's still a good eighth grade player. But he's now on the varsity team."

At least the "previous performance" argument stays in the same generation. The "inheritance" argument spans multiple generations. The theory is that if the kid's father, uncle, grandfather or some other ancestor was a good player, then the descendent kid is also a good player. In some instances genetics may be helpful, but there are also times when a kid's performance and statistics might reasonably lead to the conclusion that although the kid's father was a fine player in his day, when it comes to athletic ability either the kid favors his mother or in that family, coordination and speed are like twins in other families and skip generations. When this happens, the kid's parents and sometimes other community members may expect the coach to ignore those ugly statistical and performance things and just allocate playing time by family reputation. Sometimes the local coach, having been made aware of the kid's lineage, will go ahead and play the kid. The problem that then arises is not due to the local coach, but due to the ignorance of the opposing team's coach. Not having been informed of the kid's heritage, all he sees is what's on the court or field in front of him. Since he hasn't been told that the defender who is a few inches too short or a step slow is the son of a local athletic hero, the opposing coach naively runs plays in the defender's direction time and time again with a good deal of success. If only someone had made the opposing coach aware of this player's bloodlines, no doubt he would make better decisions.

I'm sure once you've coached for a while you'll hear players and parents make other creative arguments for playing time, but those are the main ones.

Competitively yours,
Uncle J.W.

Get With the Program

Dear Uncle J.W.,

I enjoyed your letter about playing time. You're right. Once a coach allows playing time to be based on anything other than performance, it opens up a Pandora's box. It turns all of the players and parents into lawyers. Rather than making plays, everybody's busy making their case.

In your last letter, you touched on the subject of player development and I would like you to say more about that. Even before I began coaching, I noticed that all great coaches have one thing in common – great players. A lot of programs have great players once in a while, on those odd years when the stars are in perfect alignment. But programs that really stand out are the ones that have great players year in and year out. It's not just random forces of nature at work in these programs. There's a plan in place. Programs like that aren't just relying on fate to provide talented players. They've got something they're doing to develop players year in and year out. Tell me about that. What's going on there?

Trying to get with the program,
Paul

Dear Paul,

You're correct. Even a run-of-the-mill coach, just by the grace of the law of averages, will have a year here and there where he is blessed with great players. One of the true marks of a great coach is that he doesn't have great players just every now and then, he has them continually.

Coaches who have great players year after year have great players not because fate has been kind and smiled on them, but because these coaches have put a program in place that takes players who are good and makes them great. It's not uncommon to hear spectators watching a great team say, "Any coach could win with players like that." To a degree that's true, but the greater truth is that not just any coach can put together a program that develops players like that.

In earlier letters I talked about some of the philosophical foundations of having a great program; having a program be what it is and not try to be what it is not; focusing on success and not accepting excuses; understanding that athletics are competitive and that playing time must be performance based. Now we're getting into areas that still have some philosophical aspects, but also cross over into practical aspects and process.

On rare occasions you find a gifted athlete who can step onto the field for the first time in his life during his junior or senior year and perform at a high level. But that player is the exception and not the rule. Most players, in order to become highly skilled, need to develop those skills.

Even on a team that has a reasonably good varsity coach, you may find struggling and frustrated athletes, who even though they are on the varsity team don't have varsity level skills. In frustration, these players often ask the coach, "What do I need to do?" The correct answer is "Go back in time six years and learn how to play the game."

Just because problems show up at the varsity level doesn't

mean that's where they are created. In order to avoid playing poorly when they get to the varsity level, players need to start developing skills much earlier in life. One of the secrets to having a good athletic program is recognizing the importance of the word "program." In a good athletic program, players begin learning and playing at a young age. Not only do they learn and play, they are taught and learn to play the right way.

Teaching young players the right way from the start is critical for two reasons. One, it helps them to win. As you may have gathered from my earlier letters, playing to win is nothing you should apologize for at any level. Granted, the emphasis on winning, rather than maximizing potential, can be taken to extremes and become obnoxious. However, encouraging young players to be dedicated, work hard and do things the right way and be their best both as team members and individuals and experience winning as a natural bi-product of that is something our society is better, not worse, for. When a young player learns to play the right way and experiences success early, the player enjoys that success and wants more of it. The player identifies herself as someone who is good at that sport and someone who can achieve. She's seen the results of making an effort and is therefore willing to make additional effort. On the other hand, consider what happens to a young player who isn't taught how to do things correctly. She goes into her first game and flails about on a team that gets stomped. She's not going to view that as a pleasant experience or identify herself as someone who is going to have success at that particular sport. Getting her to continue working to develop is not going to be easy.

The other drawback to teaching or allowing young players to do something incorrectly when they're starting out is that when they move up to higher levels, the higher level coach either has to allow them to continue doing things wrong or deconstruct what the player is doing and re-teach him.

The classic example of this is watching young players shoot a basketball. Due to a lack of strength, they come up with all kinds of strange ways to get the ball up to the rim. There's the two-hand, belly tuck, curl over, uncoil and fling. The one-hand, ball-behind-the-ear shot put, sometimes accompanied by the big league baseball pitching wind up. There's the two-hand, behind-the-head catapult, both backspin and topspin versions. And there's the two-hand, cram-the-ball-into-your-chest, then fire it for the rafters while simultaneously executing a standing broad jump shot favored by so many fourth grade three-point shooters.

All of these shooting techniques have one thing in common. They're grossly wrong. Any player still trying to shoot this way on a varsity team will be at best ineffective and possibly also a laughingstock. For a program to be strong, coaches need to immediately address these problems when they see them and teach the player the correct way to shoot. If that means having elementary school players shoot at an 8-foot rim, fine. The same thing can be said for passing a football, throwing a baseball or swinging a golf club. It's never too soon to teach a player the proper technique.

Not only should a coach teach a beginning player the correct way, the coach should also insist that the player execute the skill in the correct manner.

If a seventh grade player is shown that the correct way to shoot a basketball is with one hand, but the player continues to shoot with two hands the varsity coach needs to make it very clear to the player that if he's still shooting with two hands when he tries out for the varsity team he will be cut from the team on the first day. The coach should also explain why that will be the case.

If a player in seventh grade is shown how to do something correctly, yet four years later is still doing that thing incorrectly, what does that say about the player? There are really only two possibilities. Either the player is an incredibly slow learner or too stubborn to want to learn. Whichever it is, for the varsity team to be successful, players with those flaws need to be cut, the sooner the better.

Now, there are some people who will argue that telling a 12-year-old something like that is coldhearted. But when you think this through and consider the message you're sending and the potential outcomes, making it clear to the player that in this program there are requirements rather than just suggestions is not the coldhearted thing to do, but is the kindhearted thing to do.

If you show a young player the right way and let him know up front that doing things the right way is mandatory, not optional, then he can go about doing things the right way, develop and refine his skills and blossom as a player in a successful program.

If you show a young player the right way to do something, but then show indifference when he goes back to doing it the wrong way, then he will never fully develop his skills and when he gets to a higher level will either be cut from the team or more likely be among many players who do things the wrong way in a losing program. By not being honest with the player and instead letting him do things the wrong way, you're setting him up for failure.

When you look at it in that light, which is the kind thing to do and which is the cold thing to do?

Your mean old uncle,
J.W.

Correction is an Act of Love

Dear Uncle J.W.,

Yes, as I recall you could be blunt and demanding, both with younger and older players. Yet, to this day almost all of them speak fondly of you. That's always been something that struck me as being counter intuitive. This isn't 100 percent true, but more often than not it seems like coaches who are direct and don't beat around the bush in making demands end up being liked by the players while the coaches who are easier on the players are less well liked. Why is that?

I understand that as a coach, you have to make demands on players. But when some coaches make demands it's accepted and when other coaches make demands it's resented. And the difference doesn't appear to be in the tone of voice. Some coaches yell and get their point across. Others never raise their voice above a conversational level and yet get their point across. Meanwhile, other coaches are ignored no matter whether they're talking casually or screaming until they're blue in the face. What's going on there? What does it take to get players to respond to a coach?

Wanting them to listen,
Paul

Dear Paul,

I was never too big on yelling at players – although I can recall times when I raised my voice. It's not that I had any moral qualms about yelling. But from a practical perspective, most of the time I didn't think it was effective, especially if a coach yells on a regular basis.

As a coach, one of the things you have to consider is the kids' home life. Some kids come from homes where nobody ever raises their voice. Parents in those homes never yell at their kids. They have "discussions." Other kids come from homes where people yell and scream all the time. That's just the way they communicate. For a coach, regularly yelling at a player who comes from either of those types of families is usually unproductive. The player who comes from a quiet home goes into a shell like a scared turtle. Meanwhile the player from a loud home has no problem with people yelling. That rolls off him like water off a duck's back.

The conclusion I reached is that if indeed it's necessary, yelling should be saved for special occasions.

Even without ranting and raving, unless the game is chess, a coach often has to speak loudly just to be heard. Gyms, football fields, baseball diamonds and tracks are frequently spacious and loud. Those of us who spend a lot of time at such places view this as ambiance. Particularly with younger players it's necessary for a coach to explain to them that speaking loudly is not necessarily an indication of frustration or anger, it's just the practical need to be heard. Players are typically perceptive enough so that after a few practices they can tell by the tone, not the volume, of the coach's voice whether he's pleased or displeased with the way things are going.

Regardless of how loudly or softly a coach speaks, a coach must speak to players. The essence of coaching is giving players instruction, an opportunity to perform what was instructed, and feedback on how well or poorly they performed.

Some coaches give players minimal feedback. Other coaches give players a lot of feedback. It's a matter of style, but I prefer the latter, particularly early in the season. A coach should tell the player when he does something right and tell the player when he does something wrong. You don't have to be Sigmund Freud, or perhaps a better comparison would be B.F. Skinner, to figure out the psychology of this approach. Since most players find it more pleasant to hear about things they're doing right, over time they begin to do more things right and fewer things wrong. This is a coaching philosophy that's just not that complicated.

Some coaches from the emphasize-the-positive, don't-damage-fragile-self-esteem crowd are reluctant to tell players when they've done something wrong. That's another of those things that sound warm and fuzzy, but with any objective analysis is quickly revealed to be absurd. There are those who claim that all problems in life are problems of distribution. Coaches who can't bring themselves to tell players when they've done something wrong have distributed themselves on the wrong area of the sideline. They're in the coaching box, but belong over with the cheerleaders.

Consider the following situation. A coach pulls a player out the game for doing something wrong and when the player comes to the bench, instead of telling the player what he did wrong, the coach says "Good job. Good job." Why should that coach or anyone else be surprised when the player goes back into the game later and makes the same mistake that he made before? In order to spare the player's feelings the coach didn't tell the player there was a problem and he didn't tell the player how to correct the problem. In order to avoid the risk of damaging the player's self esteem by correcting him on the sideline, the coach lets the player go back out on the floor and continue to embarrass himself and the team in front of the whole crowd.

Yes, this sounds bizarre, but watch bad teams and you'll see it happen all the time.

A variation on that theme is the coach who will tell players who mess up, "Well, you tried hard." Players who have any talent and character to go along with that talent aren't comforted by a comment like that. They take it as an insult, and rightly so.

To tell a player, "Well, you tried hard," and not offer correction is equivalent to telling a player, "You tried hard…but due to either a lack of talent or not knowing what you're doing you failed. And I don't know what to tell you to correct that situation in the future."

That's a program that needs a new coach.

When players do something wrong, they need to be told what they've done wrong and how to correct it. They also need to understand that making the correction is mandatory, not optional. Coaches who can't bring themselves to do this consistently aren't sparing players' feelings, they're impeding players' progress and failing to show that they care about their players.

In the Biblical Book of Proverbs it says, "It's the child he loves that God corrects."

The concept behind the verse is not only important for the coach to understand, but it may be even more important for the player to understand.

Players need to understand that when a coach corrects a player, the coach isn't doing it for the coach's benefit, the coach is correcting the player for the player's benefit. When a coach corrects a player the coach isn't disrespecting the player, he's demonstrating belief in the player, the belief that the player has the talent and character necessary to correct the problem and improve. A player shouldn't feel insulted when a coach sees him having a problem and tells him how to correct it. The time for a player to feel insulted is when a coach sees him do something wrong, but doesn't tell him how to correct it. That's when a player needs to wonder if he still has the coach's confidence.

Not only should a coach correct a player when a player does something wrong. A coach should also take the opportunity to push a player farther even when, or especially when, a player has done something right, but not completely right.

When a player does something right, but not perfect it presents an ideal time for a coach to make a correction.

Feel free to choose your own words to fit the situation, but the message boils down to the following: "You just made a nice play and I like that. But by making this adjustment you can do even better and get closer to perfection. I'm telling you this for two reasons. As a coach, yes I am a nit-picking perfectionist. But I'm also telling you this because I think you can be not just good, but very good and I care enough about you to push you to be the absolute best player you can be."

Players will accept a lot of correction and play for a coach when they understand he's correcting and pushing them for their benefit, not his own.

It's the player he loves that a coach corrects.

Good coaches are never satisfied,
Your uncle J.W.

Building the Players
not the Problems of Tomorrow

Dear Uncle J.W.

In your last two letters, you talked about the need to put a program in place that gives players the necessary tools at lower levels so that they're ready to play at the varsity level and you talked about coaches communicating with players. But what about communication between the varsity coach and coaches of the developmental teams? Obviously, the developmental coaches are critical to the varsity team's success, yet in some schools all of the teams seem to be completely disconnected, all of them going in different directions. That makes no sense. What needs to be done to have an effective working relationship between the developmental teams and the varsity team?

Hoping to start them right,
Your nephew Paul

Dear Paul,

In some ways coaching a high school program is more complicated than coaching a college program. As a coach in a college program you can establish your system of play and recruit players who fit that system. In a high school program you get straight run players, whatever the genetics of the community provides, and that can vary from year to year. If you're a basketball coach who likes to run a post oriented offense and your community goes through a four-year dearth of tall kids you're going to have to be flexible in your offensive scheme. For a football coach the same principle applies. It's hard to run that wide open spread offense when your team is heavy on bulldozers and short on gazelles.

This means that as a high school coach you're going to need to have some flexibility. But even though you need some flexibility, you should still have a system. The flexibility is flexibility within that system.

When I talk about having a system what I'm saying is that you need to have certain core things that you do at the varsity level and every team within your program builds toward those core things. There must be a common direction. All of your lower level teams must be building blocks within the same system, not scattered and unfocused with each team doing it's own thing.

The primary purpose of every lower level team is to make the varsity team better. Each coach at the lower levels must know and accept that premise. If a lower level coach can't accept that and instead has his own agenda, then that coach needs to go be part of a different program.

As a varsity coach you need to have coaches at lower levels teaching certain core skills, offenses and defenses that are building blocks within your system. These things must be central to what they do and they're not optional. They will be done.

However, this doesn't mean coaches at lower levels are handed a script and have no latitude. Developmental level coaches also should be doing at least a couple of things that are of their own design. As a varsity coach you want to encourage creative thinking by your lower level coaches not only so they feel a greater sense of involvement, but also because they might come up with something that you like well enough to adopt at the varsity level.

At least as important as having continuity in the program, and an area even more likely to cause problems, is having an understanding of the player development goals in the younger programs.

Losing varsity programs frequently suffer due to one of two philosophical playing time mistakes made by the developmental level teams. One mistake is the everybody-plays-equal-time philosophy. The other mistake is nucleus building.

The everybody-plays-equal-time philosophy is another of those approaches popular with the warm and fuzzy crowd, but wrong.

The first and most egregious problem with everybody-plays-equal-time is that it teaches players that talent and work ethic count for nothing. It teaches young people that if you want something in life, all you have to do is show up and you're entitled to it. Can you imagine a worse lesson to be teaching a young person? How long will it be before a young person sent into the world with that mindset meets with a rude awakening?

The other thing that happens is that since it is known that everybody on the team is going to play equal time, which will lead to losing, the way to improve the chance of winning is for there to be fewer players to spread the time among. The more talented players know that the team is being held back by the less talented players and the less talented players know that they're holding the team back. Since there's no way to mitigate that by playing the more skilled players more and the less skilled players less, the only solution available is to discourage less skilled players from being on the team at all.

That's not desirable either from an ethical or practical perspective. You want broader participation at younger levels. For the kids, it's good for them to try a variety of activities at a young age. For the program, you might find a diamond in the rough.

49

The second common way that teams err in allocating playing time on younger level teams is an approach I refer to as "nucleus building." Nucleus building is the opposite extreme of equal time. Nucleus building is when coaches select the varsity team's starters while the kids are still in fifth grade. The anointed few then receive all of the attention and playing time while the rest of the players are allowed to hang around, but are generally ignored. The selected players are given every opportunity to develop and sometimes do, but sometimes don't. The other players are given no chance to develop and don't.

In a program based on nucleus building there is no Plan B. When one or more of the chosen few doesn't pan out as expected there's nobody available to step in and fill the void.

The basketball team that went undefeated in eighth grade had a 6'2" center, a quick guard and a forward who shot the lights out. But by their junior year the center hadn't grown any more, the guard never really learned to go to his left and when he filled out lost half a step. And the forward? He got arrested. Now what?

In football, the quarterback who was bigger than everyone else and looked like a man among boys when he was in seventh grade blends in pretty well now that he's a senior. In fact, when he goes back to pass and can't find any of those receivers who never developed and just pulls the ball down and tries to run over defenders like he used to, he blends in so well under all those tacklers that you can barely see him.

Oddly enough, when varsity coaches from a nucleus building program are forced to look for a replacement for one of the anointed who didn't pan out, these coaches are often surprised when the replacement doesn't play well.

"I gave the kid a chance and he just didn't perform."

Coaches in a nucleus building program ignore a kid for seven years, give him little or no instruction, finally out of desperation throw him into a game completely unprepared, and when he plays like he's unprepared, they blame him. That makes no sense.

What's the answer for determining playing time at the lower

developmental levels? Everybody-gets-equal-time doesn't work and selecting your starters early and making them the nucleus also has pitfalls, so what do you do?

Somewhere between these two extremes, there's a right place to be. It may vary from program to program and even from game to game, but there are two constants. Open and fair competition along with honesty must always be part of the program, even at younger levels.

There's nothing wrong with players even at young ages being taught that it will be necessary to compete in life. However, it needs to be made very clear that the purpose of competition, particularly among teammates, is not to destroy your teammate or allow it to destroy you. The purpose of competition is to push both you and your teammate to become better players. In competition, one player will come out ahead of the other at the end of the day. But tomorrow's another day and there's no guarantee the player who comes out ahead will be the same player every day. And we're just talking internal competition. When we add in external competition, there's nothing that says both of our players can't come out ahead of the players on the opposing teams. That's what we're looking for.

What you're attempting to do is establish a team culture that includes an understanding that everyone is expected to work hard and improve. Equal playing time is not guaranteed and playing time will be based on talent, work that is reflected in improvement, and the team's needs in any particular game. While playing time is not guaranteed, no player will be ignored and abandoned.

Even though equal playing time is not guaranteed, at developmental levels, every player at some point in the season needs to get some playing time – and meaningful playing time.

As a coach don't, particularly at younger levels, only play certain kids for short periods of time when the score is lopsided. If a kid is ever going to develop, he needs to play in at least a few spots here and there during mainstream time when the game has yet to be decided. That mainstream time may not come in the tournament finals, but not every game is the tournament finals. And if by chance fouls, illness, injuries or cruel fate demand that someone from the second string needs to step in during the tournament finals, both the coach and player are going to feel better if that's not the first time the player has been in the fire.

An argument can be made that having a routine substitution pattern might be easier, but not necessarily better. When it comes to substitutions, at any level, there's something to be said for a coach being a little unpredictable. When a player on the bench knows she's probably not going into the volleyball match until the third game she's less motivated to stay mentally focused on what's going on during the first and second games. But when that player knows that her coach has the potential to take a wild notion and send her in at any time and expect her to play like she knows what's going on, then she has a motivation to stay focused. Players on the floor also need to know that the coach isn't locked into keeping any particular people on the floor. Any player can come out at any time. Best make the most of any time that you're in the game.

Playing time allocation is always one of the most challenging aspects of coaching, particularly at the developmental team level. What you're shooting for is to create an environment: where players understand that playing time is earned, not an entitlement; where players recognize their own strengths and weaknesses and work with coaches to improve; where players understand the benefits of competition and how to go about it in an honorable way; where players are engaged and motivated physically, mentally and spiritually.

If you can establish that type of environment on teams at the younger developmental levels, you'll end up with the great players that the higher level teams need in order to be successful.

You're always more likely to end up where you want to go if you start down the right path in the first place.

Your Uncle J.W.

Responsibility & Authority Belong in the Same Place

Dear Uncle J.W.,

When you talk about starting down the right path, that implies there is more than one path and the right path must be chosen. What happens when, as a coach, you choose a path and you're confident that it is the right path, but players, parents or others want to travel a different path? What I'm getting at is the challenge that coaches face in getting others to believe in the direction that they've chosen for the program. Sometimes other people have other ideas and this can cause problems. How do I correct these problems, or better yet determine what causes them and address the causes to prevent the problems from arising in the first place?

Perplexed on this one,
Your nephew Paul.

Dear Paul,

When you talk about a coach choosing a path and players and possibly others wanting to choose a different path, what you're really talking about are the subjects of responsibility and authority. Although many people try to separate these subjects, for an athletic program to be successful responsibility and authority have to be in the same place.

If a coach is going to be given the responsibility to make an athletic program successful, he must also have the authority to make decisions and take actions necessary to make the program successful. Responsibility without authority is a recipe for failure.

Oddly enough, far too many coaches are willing to not only allow other people to usurp the authority they need, but they go beyond allowing people to usurp authority and find excuses to give it away.

One of the trademarks of many school systems that are failing both athletically and academically is that people in charge have lost sight of their role and mission and are allowing the inmates to run the prison. There are both teachers and coaches who are under the mistaken impression that their primary purpose is to entertain, rather than educate. Granted, both academic enlightenment and athletic achievement can and should be pleasant and rewarding experiences and therefore entertaining. But entertainment is incidental, not the primary goal.

People who proffer the notion that players must be entertained will support their position by saying, "The players are happy. And a happy player is a good player."

Bull! They have it in the wrong order. A good player is more likely to be a happy player.

While there are some players who would be perfectly happy to goof off and never break a sweat, there are no players who will by goofing off maximize their potential and experience the happiness that comes with winning as a result of doing the work necessary to maximize their potential. The best the entertainment crowd can hope for is creating happy losers. Far too many adults who should know better are good with that these days, but they shouldn't be and as a coach you shouldn't be.

In order to fulfill the responsibility of building and maintaining a successful program, a coach must be given the necessary authority, must retain that authority and judiciously exercise it.

While authority is necessary, it can also be dangerous, engendering resentment among those subject to the authority, and bloating the ego of the person holding the authority. To avoid either of these pitfalls it is helpful to have all parties involved understand why authority and responsibility are placed in the hands of one person rather than spread around.

To make an analogy, compare a team beginning its season with a ship setting out on a voyage to sea. On the ship, you have a captain and sailors. On a team you have a coach and players.

During the ship's voyage the captain sets the course, steers the ship and commands the sailors. If the captain knows what he's doing and capable sailors follow commands, the voyage is successful. If during the course of the voyage, some of the sailors decide they should set the course or instead of following commands ignore them or follow a different set of commands that their parents sent from home, then the voyage will not go well.

Even if the ship's captain makes some mistakes here and there, the ship stands a better chance of avoiding the rocks if the captain alone remains at the wheel as opposed to having four sailors and two stow-away parents all grab the wheel with the captain and have everybody try to steer at the same time.

For a ship to have a successful voyage the captain and sailors both must understand their roles and execute them effectively.

For a team to function properly the coach and players must also understand, accept and effectively execute their roles. The reason a coach has the authority to determine what plays are run and which players are put in the game to run them isn't to bolster the coach's ego. It's because that's the coach's role, his responsibility.

While the ultimate responsibility and authority for making decisions is with the coach, that doesn't mean the coach operates in a vacuum. Coaches can and should have back and forth communication with players. The player's role in that communication is not to make a decision to do something different, but to provide information and receive information allowing the player to better put into effect the decision that the coach has made.

Coaches and players have different roles on a team. Coaches make decisions. Players make plays. Those are separate responsibilities and neither is necessarily more important than the other. For the team to win, both things must happen. The coach has to make the correct decisions and the players have to effectively execute those decisions.

Sometimes a coach will have a player who is interested in expanding her role to include decision making. When that happens some role clarification is in order. As a coach, feel free to use your own words, but convey the following message:

"I've been playing and coaching this game for several years and was able to persuade someone that I'm smart enough to coach this team. Among the players on this team, I have you, a teenager who has some ideas about how the team should function, ideas that are contrary to mine. While I'm confident that my ideas are correct, there is a possibility, a slight possibility, that yours could be. If indeed your ideas are better than mine that would indicate that you have an exceptional mind for this game. A mind like that can't be wasted out there on the field where plays are made. A mind like that needs to be kept where the decisions are made, right here on the sidelines. Now go sit there on the bench, right at the end, so I'll know exactly where to find you if the need arises for me to consult with you about some of the ideas that you have."

Usually, you only need to have that conversation with one player and the others get the message.

Be the captain of your ship,
Your uncle J.W.

56

Terms of Participation

Dear Uncle J.W.,

What you say about a ship having only one captain makes perfect sense. But what about the sailors who choose not to board the ship or jump ship in mid voyage.

As I take over this program I'm already finding that some students who are good enough players to help the team either aren't planning to play or are waffling. I'm told that last year's team had a player quit in mid-season. A few years back in a neighboring town most of a team threatened to quit in the middle of the season.

Meanwhile, even though our school's athletic teams haven't won all that often, as long as they have enough kids out to field a team, we have administrators and school board members who talk about our athletic "participation" level as something to be proud of. As I take over and do some of the things that you've talked about and offend some people, as you've said these things will do, and as a result participation numbers drop, I suspect these administrators and board members won't be happy.

What's your advice on how to address these issues?

One hard choice always leads to another.
Your nephew Paul.

Dear Paul,

While it might seem like the questions you posed in your last letter are about kids and the character of kids in regard to athletics that's not really the case. All of the questions you asked in your last letter ultimately are about the integrity, credibility and character of adults when dealing with kids and athletics. The only way kids are involved is that they're checking to see whether the adults are serious or whether they can be bluffed and manipulated.

First, let's address the question of potential players either choosing not to participate or waffling about whether or not they're going to participate. Grieving or not grieving over players who choose not to participate is one of the things that separate rookie coaches from veterans. A rookie coach worries about who's not there. A veteran coach focuses on the players who care enough to be there. That applies not only to the player deciding whether or not to be on or not be on the team, it applies to all team activities. For example at an off season work out, if only a handful of players show up, the rookie coach frets about the ones who are absent. The veteran coach takes the opportunity to give those who are there extra individual attention and gives them the skills to become the foundation of a winning team. A good coach coaches the players who are there.

Players who waffle about whether or not they're going to play are really just trying to negotiate terms. They want to be the center of attention or hope to get some kind of special treatment. A coach needs to be especially clear to these players about the program's terms of participation. Every player in the program is required to either be all-in or all-out. There's no partial commitment. All players who are part of the team operate under the same expectations, that they are fully committed spirit, mind and body, not just one or two out of the three. If you have talent and commitment, then you're welcome to be part of the team. If you lack commitment, then it's best for both you and the team that you go in a different direction and find something else to do.

In your first couple of years as a coach you may find that under those terms some kids who have the athletic ability but lack commitment don't play. That's fine. You'll get by without their athletic ability and you'll also get by, quite nicely, without the conflict and drama that those players bring.

In the short term, this approach may reduce your player numbers. However, you'll find that after a couple of years your player numbers pick back up. Be assured there are players out there who want to participate in a successful program where there are expectations and not a lot of drama and prima donnas. When you get your program cleaned up, the players you don't want will stay away and the players that you do want will join. Note that in regard to "players you want" and "players you don't want" that there are a lot of players who can go either way. If they're playing in a program directed by adults who have high expectations, they meet them. If they're playing in a program directed by adults who have low expectations, they meet those.

Having players quit in midseason is a similar issue. Players normally attempt to use quitting as a threat. The most effective approach to dealing with this is a preemptive strike. At the beginning of the season let the players know that you don't view quitting as a threat. Tell players that if during the course of the season they decide they're going to quit, then quit, but tell them to make sure that when they quit, they also leave. There are few things worse than a player who has for all practical purposes given up and quit, but is still hanging around. If a player is going to quit and no longer make an effort to contribute, he needs to leave and get out of the way.

When a coach tells a player to go ahead and quit, the player may claim, "You don't care about me."

To that, a coach's response is, "No. I care about you. Both you and I care about you. We have that in common. Where we differ is that you care only about you. I care about you and I also care about me and the other members of the team. I'm not willing to care only about you when that is to the detriment of myself and everyone else. If you want to care only about you and not me and not the rest of the team, then your choice to remove yourself is probably a good idea. No point in staying around people you don't care about."

While we're talking about kids attempting to negotiate their own terms of participation and leaving the team this is also a good time to address the subject of players behaving irresponsibly and being either suspended or dismissed from the team.

How disciplinary situations are handled on school athletic teams is another matter that typically says more about the adults involved than it does about the kids. Athletic team disciplinary situations boil down to three phases:

*Players through improper behavior create a problem;

*Adults involved with the program (coaches, administrators board members and sometimes law enforcement) address the problem;

*Kids, not just those whose behavior created the problem, but all of them, take a message, good or bad, into life based on how adults address the problem.

Player misbehavior, like losing is often the product of a culture of tolerating or emphasizing and encouraging the wrong things. When players choose to violate established policies, they are making that choice based on one or more perceptions:

*I won't get caught.

*If I get caught, the consequences will not be severe and I will not be held fully accountable.

*If I get caught and am dismissed from the program, I don't care.

Depending on how the aforementioned adults address the situation, the perceptions the kids based their behavioral choice on are proven either valid or invalid.

It's also important to realize that the perceptions leading to the undesirable behavior typically came from somewhere. They didn't just pop into the kids' heads. Those perceptions are based on past experience, established practices the player has grown familiar with in the athletic program and perhaps in the school system in general or his home life.

In an earlier letter you talked about excuses not just coming up occasionally, but coming up so often that they seem to be a cornerstone of your athletic program. When you say things like that, what you're talking about is the culture of your athletic program, the norms and standards, how things are routinely done, what things are accepted and what things are neither accepted nor tolerated.

Policies and rules have their place and if you adopt them you should plan to follow them because if you don't you will have no credibility. However, establishing a culture that sets and enforces standards in a manner that makes proper behavior normal and expected can go a long way toward preventing players from ever conceiving the perceptions that lead to misconduct.

Perhaps some examples of team cultures, bad and good, will make this clearer.

On the way home from a road game, the team stops at a fast food restaurant. Prior to going into the restaurant the coach reminds players that they are representing the school and community and he expects them to behave accordingly. Once inside the restaurant, most of the players behave well, but a couple of them are loud and obnoxious and when they get up to go back to the bus they leave napkins and some loose French fries on the table. As the coach picks up the napkins and fries he thinks to himself, "Kids will be kids. Most of the kids behaved well. Fortunately, I've only got two like that."

Alternatively, consider the same scenario as above except when the two players start to get loud and obnoxious the coach immediately tells them to knock it off. If two players leave a mess on the table, he goes out to the bus and sends them back in to clean it up. As they clean it up, he explains to them that if there are any similar problems in the future, the two of them won't be eating in restaurants with the team. They'll wait on the bus while the rest of the team goes in and eats.

Here's another example. The team has a rule requiring extra drills for any player who isn't on time for practice. The way it's implemented, the rule applies to everyone except the star player. When that player shows up late for practice, nothing is said.

The alternative culture is that when star player shows up late, he does the drills just like everyone else.

Here's a final example. When players get on the bus to go to a road game, they all pile on like a stampede of buffalo, fling equipment randomly and during the trip not only jabber and shout, but shriek like a bunch of fifth grade girls at a pajama party and jockey from seat to seat. When they get off the bus they leave not only candy wrappers, but also some of their equipment.

The alternative is that when players get on the bus, there's no jostling. They walk up the steps, are required to greet the bus driver, store their equipment not in the aisles, but in an orderly manner. During the ride they talk, but don't shout and certainly don't shriek. When they get off the bus, they thank the bus driver. Team captains are the last ones off the bus and check to make sure all debris is cleaned up and no equipment is left on the bus.

Compare the messages that those two cultures send to players every day.

In a team with a bad culture things are allowed to slide. And if things are lax in the behavioral realm off the court, they're probably just as lax in performance on the court. Once things start sliding, they keep sliding.

In a team with a good culture there are expectations and those expectations are clear and enforced. Players on teams with a good culture understand that adults involved with the program are serious. When a player from a team with a good culture faces peer pressure to do something wrong that player faces the choice with no false perceptions. "My coach has a cow if players are loud in restaurants or leave candy wrappers on the bus. If I do what these other kids are trying to get me to do now and he gets wind of it there won't be any nudge-nudge, wink-wink, kids-will-be-kids stuff. I'll be parked on the bench with a perfect set of his dental records in the seat of my shorts."

Adults involved with high school athletic programs need to care enough about young people to send them the right message. When tested by kids, adults need to have enough backbone to be adults. In programs where corners are cut, things are allowed to slide, exceptions are made and rules are skirted or revised, the players know it, the community knows it and other teams and neighboring communities know it. Word gets out and once that credibility is lost, it's hard to restore. Worst of all, kids take that message into life with them.

An advocate of tough love.
Uncle J.W.

If Everybody's Perfect,
How Can there be Losers?

Dear Uncle J.W.

Tough love. I understand. Sometimes instead of giving people what they want, it's better to give them what they need. Some people have a real problem doing that, especially in matters involving kids. Is this something more prevalent now than in the past? You're old. You should be someone who would know the answer to that question.

I have kids who come to practice and they think they're wonderful and entitled merely because they've shown up and have a pulse. It's not that they're bad kids. It's just that they're not as perfect as they think they are. For some reason it hasn't dawned on them that they're not instantly and automatically good at everything they do. When they try something new and they're not immediately adept at it, they either give up or get frustrated. Or they're completely delusional and think they're good even when they're not. Where does this attitude come from and as a coach, how do I deal with it?

Perplexed among the perfect.
Your nephew Paul.

Dear Paul,

We are in the age of perceived entitlement, those who think they deserve much for doing little. This is an epidemic among the young, but only because it has been taught to them by the adults in their lives. When the shepherds lose their way, it should come as no surprise that the sheep are lost.

In an earlier letter I talked about teachers and coaches sometimes forgetting that their primary role is to educate rather than to entertain. While there is nothing wrong with education being entertaining, it is wrong to allow entertainment to become an objective that pushes education into the background, or in some instances completely off the stage.

In the matter we're addressing here, we have a similar problem. While providing things for and encouraging young people are commendable behaviors and part of being a caring adult, both of these behaviors can be done incorrectly or overdone to the detriment of those who the adults are trying to help.

Children who receive rewards and are constantly told they are special and wonderful merely because they exist, won't be inspired to do much more in life than exist. Instead, they grow up believing they deserve to receive rewards, acclaim and anything else their little hearts desire merely because they exist.

Some of the most successful coaches, parents and teachers aren't always the most eloquent people. Instead of using long words such as "deserve" and "entitled," they use short, four-letter words such as "work" and "earn."

As previously noted, in competitive athletics they keep score and there are wins and losses. Some scores are better than others and some teams win and some teams lose. For adults and children who believe that every child is perfect in his or her own way, this winning and losing stuff and the differentiation that inescapably goes with it can be difficult things to get their minds around.

For children who have been routinely told that they're good at whatever they do, coming into an athletic program and having a coach tell them that they're not naturally good at something and will only get better by putting in a lot of time and effort is a whole new way of looking at life. Often enough their parents are also discomforted by this revelation.

As if that wasn't enough, once the player accepts the idea that improvement will require effort the next thing she discovers is that even with effort, improvement isn't always immediate.

Here's an odd paradox. While improvement isn't always immediate, often times the lower the level of the player's skills to start with, the sooner improvement can be seen. If a player is doing almost everything wrong, a coach can normally fix a couple of the main problems and the player will improve noticeably.

A different challenge is presented when a player has some ability, is doing some things right, but not others, and is having at least a degree of success. When a coach changes something the moderately successful player is doing, not only might that player not experience immediate improvement, but due to the change he might initially go backward for a short time.

Improvement in athletic skills and many other aspects of life often is not linear. We go from plateau to plateau. We reach one plateau and get comfortable there. If we get too comfortable, we stay there and never move to a higher plateau. If we are motivated, after stabilizing at one plateau our next ambition is to strive for a higher plateau, to take our game to the next level.

In making the transition from one plateau to the next plateau, it's not uncommon for there to be a brief period of time when a player not only doesn't get better, but temporarily gets worse. For example, consider what can happen when a basketball player makes an adjustment to shoot the ball a different way, or a quarterback holds the ball a different way, or a shot putter modifies his footwork. The basketball player may be able to make 60 percent of his free throws using his current method, but with the new method can reach 75 percent. The quarterback may be able to throw accurately out to 35 yards with his current grip, but could go to 45 with the adjusted grip. The shot putter may be looking to go from 48 to 54 feet. But when the change is first made the shooting percentage may drop to 55 percent, the passing distance to 30 yards and the shot put to 45 feet. That's temporary due to these athletes coming out of their comfort zone. Once they push through the adjustment period they will establish a new and higher comfort zone, that 75 percent, 45 yards or 54 feet.

"Comfort zone." That's a critical term. Why do adults provide things to young people too easily and reward them too much for too little? Why do players choose to pretend that mediocrity is acceptable, rather than changing techniques and working harder?

Adults are reluctant to push kids out of their comfort zone and kids are reluctant to leave their comfort zone. So everyone pretends that the comfort zone is good enough, all that needs to be asked for or worked toward. In losing programs, people may not be happy with the results, but despite that many of them are in comfort zones that are primarily responsible for those results.

As a coach trying to turn around a chronically losing program, one of the most difficult tasks you face is convincing players, parents and sometimes even yourself that it's not just all right, but necessary to get out of comfort zones.

When players practice, they sometimes will and should make mistakes. If the mistake is due to lack of attention or effort, that's a problem and the coach should address it. But if a player is going through a drill and makes a mistake because she's gone beyond her comfort zone and made changes in an effort to push herself to a higher plateau, that's not a problem. That player doesn't need to be chastised. That player needs to be encouraged to stick with it and stay the course.

When adults reward and praise kids for doing nothing, they end up with kids who are good at doing nothing. When adults reward and praise kids who are willing to come out of their comfort zone, work, earn and achieve they get kids who succeed both in athletics and in life.

Too many people in current society have become shortsighted and fail to understand the role that temporary discomfort plays in life. Getting out of a comfort zone and experiencing some temporary discomfort is often part of challenging yourself and moving forward to bigger and better things. Successful coaches aren't afraid to challenge players and push them out of their comfort zone. Players who are successful aren't afraid to accept that challenge. Parents who care about their children and their children's long term success in life shouldn't be afraid or object to seeing their child experience some temporary discomfort. Rather than trying to help their child find a way to avoid it, they should encourage the player to work through it.

A good coach is always pushing to be better,
Your uncle J.W.

The Reality of Athletes' Parents

Dear Uncle J.W.,

It doesn't surprise me to hear you say that many people have lost sight of the benefit of discomfort. Today everybody wants the easy way. If you have the slightest headache, don't let your body run a temperature and get rid of the illness, take a pill. If you're overweight, don't decrease your calorie intake and exercise, take another pill or wear a body shaping garment. It's crazy.

At the end of your last letter you talked about parents. No discussion of coaching high school athletics would be complete without talking about the role of parents. Granted, in previous letters you touched on parents and other adults now and then, but I'd like you to devote a letter specifically to parents, their role in the program and how I, as a coach, should deal with them.

Would you do that? Please.
Your nephew Paul.

Dear Paul,

Ah yes, parents. When coaches are among themselves they talk a lot about parents. Every coach has stories of parents who ranged from nuisance to nightmare.

As a coach, you will end up dealing with at least a few parents who are…to put it kindly "disagreeable." However, even though you will have some parents who are a pain and they will stand out in your memory and be the ones that you tell stories about, keep in mind that most parents a coach deals with are good people, generally supportive and often helpful to your program. Don't let a few bad ones spoil your view of the entire breed.

Some coaches feel that the less interaction they have with parents, the better. One reason cited for this is that parents are never unbiased. Even though they may make claims to the contrary, parents are always partial toward their own kids.

Personally, I put that a different way. While many parents are partial toward their own kids, other parents are unduly harsh when judging their own kids. I think the most accurate assessment is that all parents tend to focus on their own kids. As a coach, I never held that against parents. When there are a dozen or more players on a team, yet among those players only one sleeps at your house and hits you up every week for lunch money it's only logical that's the player that you as a parent will focus upon. As a coach, your best move is to understand and accept the reality that parents are going to focus on their own kids. However, you should tell parents that while there's nothing wrong with parents focusing on their own kids, it is not acceptable for them to focus on their own kids in ways that are detrimental to other players because those players are someone's kids too. The basic message is that parents are welcome to focus on their own kids, but they also need to respect the other parents and kids and not plan on having that focus become a problem for the coach or anyone else on the team. If a parent can't operate under that premise, then they shouldn't have their kid playing a team sport.

Some coaches have closed practices and don't want parents anywhere near the field or court when practices are taking place. Other coaches, sometimes as a requirement of their school, have all practices open. I think that the closed versus open practice issue shouldn't be viewed so much in context of a rule, but more as a matter of philosophy, a philosophy that should be discussed by the coach during a parent meeting prior to the season.

The philosophy I operated under was that although I didn't want parents coming in and sitting through practices day after day, I had no problem with parents stopping by for a few minutes. If they were picking up their kids from practice, they shouldn't feel they have to sit in the car or stand in the hallway. They should feel welcome to sit in the bleachers and watch the last few minutes of practice.

There were a couple of reasons that I didn't want parents sitting through entire practices day after day. First, it puts undue pressure on their kid. Second, it normally indicates that the parent isn't viewing athletic participation as something that is being done to benefit the kid's life, but is instead viewing the kid's athletic participation as something that is being done to benefit the parent's life.

A parent should feel pride in and take pleasure in their child's participation in high school athletics, but that pride and pleasure should come in the right form, or to be more accurate the right tense. The pride and pleasure that a parent derives from their child's experience in high school athletics must be geared toward the present and future, not toward the past.

Some people subscribe to what I refer to as the "glory days mentality." These people view the years spent in high school, often with an exaggerated emphasis on high school athletics, as the best and most wonderful years of a person's life, the "glory days." For people with this point of view, once they graduate from high school, life is never quite as good so the best they can do is look forward to their children getting into high school, which provides an opportunity to vicariously relive their own "glory days" through their children. The teenage athlete's experience in the present allows these parents to relive a part of their lives from the past.

Personally, I don't subscribe to the glory days mentality. I find it depressing to think that some people feel life peaks at 18 years old. I prefer a philosophy that is oriented to the future.

High school athletics, and the high school stage of life in general, at their best provide knowledge, lessons and experiences that give the teenager a foundation to build upon in the future. Earlier, I wrote of some of those building blocks: work ethic, teamwork, a sense of belonging, self-sacrifice, dedication to improvement.

These are all things that parents should want for their kids. When a teenager absorbs these lessons from high school athletics, a parent should be proud of their child and take pleasure in knowing that the teenager is absorbing lessons from both the program and the parent that are preparing that player for success in the future.

It should be pointed out that when you look at it in that light and value those kinds of benefits, those benefits are available to all members of the team and all parents no matter if the kid is the star player or the last one into the game. Being a star on the high school team is no guarantee of future success in life. Being able to absorb information and learn from others, find a role that allows you to make a contribution, push yourself to maximize your potential, conduct yourself in a manner that others respect, these are the things that are indicators of future success in life. When parents look to see if their children are learning these things and look to the future, there's more validity to the pride they take in their child's participation in high school athletics.

As long as parents operate with that understanding, there not only isn't a problem with them feeling welcome and watching a few minutes of practice now and then, there are some advantages. First, as a coach you should be running a program where you have nothing to hide, where you're not doing anything that you aren't willing to have parents see. Second, when parents see parts of a practice first hand, they learn things. Rather than getting information filtered through their kid or other kids, they get information directly and can form their own opinions. Some of the more perceptive parents will also pick up on some of the skills you're teaching and hopefully discuss them and reinforce them with their child.

While the "glory days" mentality and attempting to vicariously relive athletic triumphs from days gone by isn't desirable behavior, that doesn't mean that athletics can't be a shared experience between player and parent. When a basketball player practices shooting, she gets a lot more shots in and can do more game-like catch-and-shoot if dad or mom rebounds and passes the ball. Dad may not be able to sprint around the bases any more, but he can still hit groundballs and drop baseballs into a pitching machine. When dad passes a football, he doesn't need to throw a tight spiral. He just needs to be able to catch the ball and throw it back.

This can end up being parent-teenager quality time and help foster some warm and memorable exchanges.

"Son, you're really shooting the ball well tonight."

"Thanks mom. And with all the running around and rebounding I think you're starting to lose weight."

Unfortunately, not all parents go this direction. Some can be a pain and when they get frustrated may decide to engage you as a coach in a conversation that's not warm. Thus, the question that every coach eventually has to deal with: how do you handle an angry parent?

First of all, take preemptive measures. This is another one of those areas where an ounce of prevention is worth a pound of cure.

Prior to the start of the season have a parent meeting and make it clear how the program operates. If there will be games where not every player plays, say that. In earlier letters I talked about policies regarding playing time, missed practices etc. In the preseason meeting, lay those all out for the parents. Earlier, I talked about telling players that if they choose to quit the team, go ahead, but make sure that if they quit they also leave. A similar preemptive statement should be made to parents. Explain how your program operates and the expectations and then tell the parents, "If this doesn't work for you, then you may wish to take your child out of the program now and participate in another activity."

That may seem a bit harsh and direct, but a little harshness and directness prior to the season can go a long way to avoiding drama during the season.

Communicate with players. Every player should know their strengths and weaknesses and coaches should be working with players to correct those weaknesses. If a player is not getting game time because of a weakness, the player should know what that weakness is and be working on it. If a player is sitting on the bench as discipline for doing something wrong, the player should be told prior to the discipline taking place what he did wrong and what the expectations are for future behavior. For a coach to discipline a player out of the blue without telling the player what the discipline is for and what corrective measures are required is inviting hostility and confrontation.

If a player is aware of weaknesses or problems and working on correcting them, things will be headed in a good direction. Ideally, before going off on a coach, a parent will first talk to their kid. If a player is in suspense and frustrated, the parent will be even more lost and frustrated and a conversation between the two won't help.

If a parent has questions and the player has answers then a conflict between the parent and coach may be avoided. Granted, sometimes communicating with the player doesn't help. Either the parent doesn't ask the player, but goes straight to the coach or the player doesn't give the parent a straight answer or the parent is just mad and determined to confront the coach.

At this point, the preemptive measures have failed and as a coach you have a parent complaining to you. What do you do? How do you respond?

My advice is to keep in mind that the objective of your response is not to be offensive or defensive. Just be honest, calm and firm. Your goal isn't to put the parent in their place or defend your decisions.

If it is a disciplinary matter, tell the parent, "This was the problem. This is what I've decided to do to correct it. Part of my responsibility as a coach is to make decisions such as this. This may not be pleasant for you, your child or me, but I fulfill my responsibilities and I've made the decision. I've already talked with your child about where we go from here."

If the issue is playing time, your answer is similar. "It is my responsibility as a coach to make decisions that are in the best interest of the team, not individuals. I base my decisions on what will give our team the best opportunity to win. Sometimes players and parents may not agree with my decisions, but the decisions remain "my decisions.""

If the player has shortcomings that are keeping her on the bench tell the parent what those shortcomings are and what's being done to correct them.

Your objective in a conversation with a hostile parent isn't to berate them and it isn't to appease them. It also isn't to get into a protracted debate. Listen to their position and explain your position. If they offer pertinent information that you don't have, listen to it. If you have pertinent information that they don't have, provide it. Then go on with your day.

If after a discussion with a parent, you find you've made a mistake, correct it. But if you're comfortable with your decision, stand by it.

With all of this said, keep in mind that the vast majority of parents aren't a problem. While most coaches can name parents who were difficult to deal with, most can name a far greater number of parents who were a pleasure to deal with and who rather than creating dissension became a part of the team family.

As always, an advocate of direct communication,
Your Uncle J.W.

Tactics: Do What You Do Really Well

Dear Uncle J.W.,

As I look back on our correspondence I find we've spent almost no time talking about tactics, strategies and x's and o's. Does that mean these things are unimportant? If they are important, what do I do about them? What's a playbook without plays? Instead of talking about plays and strategy first like most coaches do, you and I are talking about them last. But I figure better late than never. You talked about avoiding being offensive or defensive when dealing with parents, but what kind of offense or defense do you recommend that I use against opponents?

Looking to expand the playbook,
Your nephew Paul.

Dear Paul,

It's not as though x's and o's aren't important. They just aren't all-important or of primary importance. I think we've taken the correct approach in talking about other things first. The things we've talked about are the foundation, best to have the foundation in place before constructing the house.

A lot of new coaches, when they're first hired, do as you've done. They scramble around reading books, watching DVDs, attending coaching clinics and talking to other coaches in search of the perfect offense or defense. Even some veteran coaches seem to change their offense and defense every year, always looking for the next big thing.

I encourage coaches, both young and old, to do research and acquire and constantly expand their base of knowledge. I also see nothing wrong with adding some wrinkles to freshen up the things your team does and keep from getting stale or predictable. Most games change and your team needs to keep up with these changes. However, the search for the perfect offense or defense is in the end destined to be about as successful as the search for the fountain of youth.

If there was only one offense or defense that teams could win with, then all great teams would be running the same offense or defense. But if you look around, that's not the case. In college basketball, championships have been won by run-and-gun teams and championships have been won by teams that depend on a half-court structured offense. In football some teams win with a passing game, others emphasize defense and the running game.

Games evolve and there are fads and trends. One team wins with a particular offense and a bunch of other teams rush to imitate. What the imitator teams neglect is that at the same time offensive coaches are figuring out how to imitate the new wave offense, defensive coaches are figuring out ways to stop it. By the time the imitator teams learn the hot, new offense, it's no longer the hot, new offense and defenses have made adjustments to stop it.

If you take a broad view and look at various winning teams over time and the different strategies, offenses and defenses they employed, there's only one logical conclusion. When it comes to offense and defense, the important thing isn't so much what you do, the important thing is that you do whatever it is that you do extremely well.

Some offenses and defenses may be better suited to certain teams and situations, but no matter what offense or defense you run, if you do it the wrong way or half-hearted it won't work very well. Diligent preparation and precise execution win more games than brilliant tactics.

Granted, tactics, strategy and matching the proper schemes to available talent have their place. A good coach puts his players in situations where they can be successful.

As I mentioned earlier, in high school, unlike college, you can't recruit talent to match your system. However, you can work with players and coaches at younger levels to develop talent that matches your system.

There are a couple of matters that are important regardless of the offense or defense that you choose.

Even though the important thing isn't what you do, but that whatever you do is something that you do extremely well, that still doesn't mean it's acceptable to be one-dimensional. One area of great strength does not excuse multiple areas of weakness. A football team that has a great running game should still be able to pass. They may not pass often, but when they need to do it, they must be able to do it. The same with a basketball team that likes to run. They also need to have a half-court offense. A hockey team with a great defense still needs to be able to score goals.

The idea is to do some things well and other things better.

A team's playbook should always contain more than you'll ever run in a given season. However, the number of things in the playbook that you use should be exactly as much as the players are

81

able to absorb – not more, not less.

There is a core within the playbook that players must learn and perfect. Once they perfect the core there must always be greater challenges available when they are prepared for them. Players need to know that there's no ceiling for them. There's always more they can learn, more they can do and they can always get better. Your message to them as a coach is that you will gladly take them as far as they're willing and able to go. Never put a lid on a player's potential.

That's about all I have to say about x's and o's. Once you select an offense or defense that you want to run, then you can consult books and DVDs and other coaches for the finer points. But those are just the frosting on the cake.

What we've talked about in these letters are the attitudes, approaches and philosophies that create a culture where doing things the right way isn't the exception, it's expected, required and normal. It's just how things are done, the little things and the big things.

We've discussed how to prepare the garden, build the soil, pull the weeds, prepare and nurture the young plants. As any gardener will tell you, once you've got the conditions right, the plants will grow. But if the soil and the other conditions are wrong, it doesn't matter what you plant, not much will grow. This is where so many coaches get frustrated. They're trying to grow a program in conditions where a program just won't grow. First, get the conditions right, then you can plant almost any crop and it will flourish.

Retired and farmed out to the garden,
Uncle J.W.

Why Coach?

Dear Uncle J.W.,

I think I'm getting the picture. In reading what you've written I've developed a vision of what I want the program to become. But I get the impression that this isn't going to happen overnight and that it won't be easy. When I recall watching you and your teams when I was a child, I only remember the victories and the celebrations. However, I'm sure there must have been hard times for you and there will be hard times for me. During the hard times, what carried you through? When the hard times come for me, what should I keep in mind, what should I cling to? Is this coaching stuff worth the time and vexation? Life is short and a person never has enough time to do everything. A person must pick and choose which things to do. What makes coaching the right choice?

Still looking for support,
your nephew Paul

Dear Paul,

It's time I made a confession. When I agreed to share any knowledge I have in order to assist you in building your program, you probably thought that was due to our family relationship and because you're my favorite nephew. Sorry to burst your bubble, but that wasn't what motivated me.

High school athletics can lay a foundation of habits and ethics that benefit an athlete not only physically, but also in matters of character and citizenship. Unfortunately, the way many high school programs currently operate instead of teaching young people how to achieve, they teach young people how to be comfortable when they underachieve and as a consequence the program underachieves and the players go forth in life and continue to underachieve. This isn't good for the players, parents, coaches or society as a whole.

While my era of coaching has passed, I believe there are values and enduring principles that are as relevant today as they were in the era in which I coached. To my dismay, over the past several decades these values have been gradually twisted into something far different than what they should be.

Dark forces of mediocrity have commandeered noble goals such as building self-confidence through hard work and achievement and perverted these objectives into receiving awards and flattery based on excuses and a false sense of entitlement.

The forces of mediocrity make a nice first impression. They look and sound friendly and helpful, wrapped in phrases such as, "It's all about the kids. They need to have fun and be happy."

Such phrases are forces of mediocrity code that ranslate into:

*The only matters of importance are that kids are comfortable and believe they're doing well.

*Don't challenge kids with demands and expectations. That

causes stress.

*Don't expose young athletes to the reality that some people are born with more talent and aptitude for certain endeavors. That might make some kids feel inferior.

*When players make mistakes, don't correct them or hold them accountable. They're just kids.

*Don't tell kids that improvement and success require work and that the consequences of not working are often disappointment and failure. That's too negative.

If the forces of mediocrity prevail, instead of learning how to win and succeed, players learn how to lose and be comfortable losers. They go forth in life not with a work ethic, but with a delusion that whatever they want is owed to them. When they inevitably discover that all the things they feel they are owed are not forthcoming, they're no longer happy. They're lost and frustrated. They suffer and the society in which they find it difficult to be productive members also suffers.

Rather than seeking short-term player happiness based on delusion you and every other coach, teacher or influential adult in a young person's life must teach young people not how to be comfortable losers, but teach them characteristics and principles that while not as popular and trendy, take them to a better place in life. You must take a stand and fight the forces of mediocrity and teach players not only the necessity, but the desirability of working hard and smart, the importance of accepting instruction from those who care about you and not only allowing others to hold you accountable, but holding yourself accountable.

When players are taught these things, they not only win in athletics they go into life prepared to do the things required to be successful. The players become productive citizens to the benefit of both themselves and society.

I realize that purveyors of the forces of mediocrity quite likely will brand me an overzealous, Neanderthal, win-at-all-cost heretic for the things I've told you in these letters. When you asked me for advice I could have written to you of x's and o's, which is probably what you expected. I could have begged off, held my peace and stayed quietly retired. But you are a young coach and have yet to be co-opted into believing that the present day naked emperors of high school athletics wear clothes. This presents an opportunity for me to help you, and by helping you help the athletes that you coach, and by helping them help society. With that much on the line to be gained or lost, even at risk of offending some or many, I and anyone else who truly care about young people and the future should not remain silent. We have a moral obligation to speak out, to rise and say a few words in defense of excellence.

You coach to make it better
Your uncle,
J.W.

www.ingramcontent.com/pod-product-compliance
Lightning Source LLC
Chambersburg PA
CBHW071825020426
42331CB00007B/1605